To Lorna

D1419664

The Phoenix Living Poets

THE SUN MY MONUMENT

THE SUN
MY MONUMENT

by
LAURIE LEE

CHATTO AND WINDUS

THE HOGARTH PRESS
1961

Published by
Chatto and Windus Ltd
with The Hogarth Press Ltd
42 William IV Street
London WC2

Clarke, Irwin and Co Ltd
Toronto

First published in
The New Hogarth Library, 1944
Second impression (re-set) 1961

Contents

Poem: 'The evening, the heather' 11
Larch Tree 12
A Moment of War 13
Words Asleep 15
Port of Famagusta 16
Music in a Spanish Town 18
Winter, 1939–1940 19
November 20
The Armoured Valley 21
At Night 22
Song in August, 1940 23
Juniper 24
Look into Wombs 25
Landscape 26
Time of Anxiety 27
Song in Midsummer 28
Stones and Scorpions 29
The Return 30
Seafront 32
Asleep we are Divided 33
Poem in the Country 34
The Three Winds 35
Equinox 36
Song in the Morning 37
End of a Season 38
Parting 39
Poem of Spring and War 40

Contents

Interval   41
Deliverance   42
Village of Winter Carols   44
Diversion   46
Milkmaid   47
Guest of Honour   48
Guadalquivir   50
The Wild Trees   51
The Multitudinous Lamp   53
River   54
The Long War   56

Acknowledgments are due to the editors of the following periodicals: *New Writing and Daylight, Penguin New Writing, Horizon, Tribune, The Listener,* and *Poets of Tomorrow 3*; in which the majority of these poems first appeared.

L.L.

Poem

The evening, the heather,
the unsecretive cuckoo
and butterflies in their disorder,
not a word of war as we lie
our mouths in a hot nest
and the flowers advancing.

Does a hill defend itself,
does a river run to earth
to hide its quaint neutrality?
A boy is shot with England in his brain,
but she lies brazen yet beneath the sun,
she has no honour and she has no fear.

Larch Tree

Oh, larch tree with scarlet berries
sharpen the morning slender sun
sharpen the thin taste of September
with your aroma of sweet wax and powder delicate.

Fruit is falling in the valley
breaking on the snouts of foxes
breaking on the wooden crosses
where children bury the shattered bird.

Fruit is falling in the city
blowing a woman's eyes and fingers
across the street among the bones
of boys who could not speak their love.

I watch a starling cut the sky
a dagger through the blood of cold,
and grasses bound by strings of wind
stockade the sobbing fruit among the bees.

Oh, larch tree, with icy hair
your needles thread the thoughts of snow
while in the fields a shivering girl
takes to her breasts the sad ripe apples.

A Moment of War

It is night like a red rag
drawn across the eyes

the flesh is bitterly pinned
to desperate vigilance

the blood is stuttering with fear.

O praise the security of worms
in cool crumbs of soil
flatter the hidden sap
and the lost unfertilized spawn of fish!

The hands melt with weakness
into the gun's hot iron

the body melts with pity

the face is braced for wounds
the odour and the kiss of final pain.

O envy the peace of women
giving birth and love like toys
into the hands of men!

The mouth chatters with pale curses

the bowels struggle like a nest of rats

the feet wish they were grass
spaced quietly.

O Christ and Mother!

But darkness opens like a knife for you
and you are marked down by your pulsing
  brain

and isolated

and your breathing,

your breathing is the blast, the bullet,
and the final sky.
Spanish Frontier, 1937.

Words Asleep

Now I am still and spent
and lie in a whited sepulchre
breathing dead

but there will be
no lifting of the damp swathes
no return of blood
no rolling away the stone

till the cocks carve sharp
gold scars in the morning
and carry the stirring sun
and the early dust to my ears.

Andalucia, 1936.

Port of Famagusta

The sun cries through his fingers
to a herd of scarlet asses,
and the green horizon throws
shutters on the oranges.

Crooning by the water's edge
the cabaret prepares her nest,
hatching hollow eggs of lust
from the dancers' painted dust.

And the harlot walks alone
like a rumour through the street,
her buttocks bright as swinging lamps,
her smile as old as stone.

With the archways full of camels
and my ears of crying zithers
how can I resolve the cipher
of your occidental heart?

How can I against the city's
Syrian tongue and Grecian door
seek a bed to reassemble
the jigsaw of your western love?

Prayers falling from the mosque
scatter wide their fruitless bones
lost among the gramophone's
lush electric evensong.

And the moon up from the sea
climbs the beanstalk of the night
while the stars like dominoes
string their tables through the sky.

Cyprus, 1939.

Music in a Spanish Town

In the street I take my stand
with my fiddle like a gun against my shoulder,
and the hot strings under my trigger hand
shooting an old dance at the evening walls.

Each saltwhite house is a numbered tomb
its silent window crossed with blood;
my notes explode everywhere like bombs
when I should whisper in fear of the dead.

So my fingers falter, and run in the sun
like the limbs of a bird that is slain,
as my music searches the street in vain.

Suddenly there is a quick flutter of feet
and children crowd about me,
listening with sores and infected ears,
watching with lovely eyes and vacant lips.

Cordoba, 1936.

Winter, 1939–1940

A gentle dove the icicle is now,
shells cannot pierce
the arctic plating of the wind,
tanks are admonished by the snow.

Let me embrace this friendly cold,
it is the final glance of love;
no more, this century, may I
have eyes or blood to know it by.

Let me with vaporizing breath
speak to my woman, while the frost
makes up a grim metallic bed
for me, and summer's broken head.

For soon the primrose sun will show
and burn with sparking trumpet flowers
this winter's flag of truce;
and passion, then, will have another use.

November

November loosens the tongue
like a leaf condemned,
and calls through the sharp blue air
a sad dance and a dread of winter.

The mistletoe reveals a star
in the dark crab-apple,
and chestnuts join their generations
under the spider sheets of cold.

I hear the branches snap their fingers
and solitary grasses crack,
I hear the forest open her dress
and the ravens rattle their icy wings.

I hear the girl beside me rock
the hammock of her blood
and breathe upon the bedroom walls
white dust of Christmas roses.

And I think; do you feel the snow,
love, in your crocus eyes,
do you watch from your trench of slumber
this blue dawn dripping on a thorn?

But she smiles with her warm mouth
in a dream of daisies,
and swings with the streaming birds
that chorus among the chimneys.

The Armoured Valley

Across the armoured valley trenched with light,
cuckoos pump forth their salvoes at the lark,
and blackbirds loud with nervous song and flight
shudder beneath the hawk's reconnaissance:
Spring is upon us, and our hopes are dark.

For as the petal and the painted cheek
issue their tactless beauties to the hour,
we must ignore the budding sun and seek
to camouflage compassion and ourselves
against the wretched icicles of war.

No festival of love will turn our bones
to flutes of frolic in this month of May,
but tools of hate shall make them into guns
and bore them for the piercing bullet's shout
and through their pipes drain all our blood away.

Yet though by sullen violence we are torn
from violet couches as the air grows sweet,
and by the brutal bugles of retreat
recalled to snows of death, yet Spring, repeat
your annual attack, pour through the breach
of some new heart your future victories.

At Night

I think at night my hands are mad,
for they follow the irritant texture of darkness
continually carving the sad leaf of your mouth
in the thick black bark of sleep.

And my finger-joints are quick with insanity,
springing with lost amazement
through a vast waste of dreams
and forming frames of desire
around the thought of your eyes.

By day, the print of your body
is like a stroke of sun on my hands,
and the choir of your blood
goes chanting incessantly
through the echoing channels of my wrists.

But I am lost in my hut
when the stars are out,
for my palms have a catlike faculty of sight,
and the surface of every minute
is a swinging image of you.

Song in August, 1940

Pondering your scented skull
I seek its antique song of peace:
    desires uncovered by your tide
    are trembling reeds with sea-blue voices.

I wind my hands around your head
and blow the hollow flute of love,
    but anger sprouts among the leaves
    and fields grow sharp with war.

Wheat bleeds upon a wind of steel
and ivy splits the poisoned sky,
    while wasps that cannot fertilize
    dive at the open flowers of men.

Your lips are turreted with guns,
and bullets crack across your kiss,
    and death slides down upon a string
    to rape the heart of our horizon.

Juniper

Juniper holds to the moon
a girl adoring a bracelet;
as the hills draw up their knees
they throw off their jasmine girdles.

You are a forest of game,
a thought of nights in procession,
you tread through the bitter fires
of the nasturtium.

I decorate you to a smell of apples,
I divide you among the voices
of owls and cavaliering cocks
and woodpigeons monotonously dry.

I hang lanterns on your mouth
and candles from your passionate crucifix,
and bloody leaves of the virginia
drip with their scarlet oil.

There is a pike in the lake
whose blue teeth eat the midnight stars
piercing the water's velvet skin
and puncturing your sleep.

I am the pike in your breast,
my eyes of clay revolve the waves
while cirrus roots and lilies grow
between our banks of steep embraces.

Look into Wombs

Look into wombs and factories and behold
nativities unblessed by hopeful stars,
the sleek machine of flesh,
the chubby bomb,
lying together in one dreadful cradle.

We are no longer ignored
in this easy agony of creation;
kings mark our breathing with a cross
and grant us honour undesired,
our vulnerability knows the trick of slaughter,
our pulse the useful trump of death.

This world, this comfortable meadow,
gay with surprise and treasure,
is common now with harvests of despair;
and mouths eager to sing,
to taste the many flowers of love,
open to tongues of bullets
and moan their shattered palates on the ground.

Landscape

The season does not leave your limbs,
like a covered field you lie,
and remembering the exultant plough
your sheltered bosom stirs
and whispers warm with rain.

Waiting does not leave your eyes,
your belly is as bright as snow
and there your naked fingers
are spread over the dark flowers
shaking out their roots.

My kiss has not yet left your blood
but slumbers in a stream
within your quiet caves:
listening to the sun it will cry forth,
and burst with leaves, and blossom with a name.

Time of Anxiety

The snowdrops make a sharp white sound,
percussions of frost on the crow black earth,
or bells for children in their steeple fingers
rung for the eyes to echo like a church.

And I am most human again with love,
most full of pity, most strange with joy,
but my thighs are full of incendiary wings
and the smoking tulips of distant summer.

In her scabbard of snow the girl conceals
magnolia flesh on a sword of bees,
but at my touch a blackbird flies
out of her breast to alarm the air.

O time of anxiety packed tight in the skull,
though courage shall break your petals of iron,
our visions are held in the gloves of death
which capture this sun and its splendid heaven.

Yet love is still human as we embrace
her haunches gambling with generations,
gambling with spring and unpredictable roots,
with furrows for wheat, or poppies of disaster.

Song in Midsummer

The day fell like a shattered city,
the stars uncovered their secret eyes,
and silence crossed the black sand
of your hair.

  With my fingers I resolved you
  disturbing the tradition of your limbs
  (the moon sprang far away)
  our mouths were gathered as fruit in the darkness,
  our arms made prophecies.

Embracing like a fugue
we sank our roots of weariness
and lay with legendary grief.

  Stems of rain grew from the hills
  opening blue petals in your throat,
  dawn went through the branches of the sky
  folding torn leaves about your sleeping breath.

Stones and Scorpions

All rinsed with sun and yet
having no flesh to hold it,
like skeletons in a noose
we hang from this brilliant summer.

Behind the sea-wire of our eyes
the petrol-hearted tigers breed,
their fatal jaws consuming all
our tears and tricks and artifice.

So agile now, their flaming tracks
dance with our sins across the world
and picking up each word of grief
scream back our madness in our ears.

What vanity preferred to lose
the simpler tongue, the rhyme of peace,
to learn this glutted speech of blood,
this doggerel drunk with too much pain?

O summer's lotus of delight
still spreads its spicy banquet down,
yet still we feed and choke upon
the stone and scorpion of war.

And still the silver star remains
pointing the cradle of the dove,
and still the harvest moon shines down
upon the world we will not have.

The Return

Starlings cover the walls with ivy
but I shout aloud and cut them down
and my love approaches among the yew trees
wearing the afternoon like a copper helmet.

She twists her curls and yellow earrings
and steps like a heron among the grasses
the leaves on her shoulders shine like feathers
and the yew tree is red under its skin.

The day she observed her limbs enchanted
she walked by the chapel with painted eyes
and bribed all the beggars and wept in secret
filling her blouse with the mask of a boy.

And the day I observed that I was a lover
I crossed the frontier to seek a wound
and fell with a fever above the Bahia de Rosas
letting the mad snow spit in my eyes.

I put her picture against the mountain
I covered the snowdrift with her scarf
and lay with her name across my haunches
chopping the ice in a fit of love.

But she tore her bed with nails of waiting
and cursed the primrose in the lamp
and loosed her kisses like pigeons for me
till they fell exhausted into another's mouth.

O come to the brambles and burning hazels
and show me your blouse with its beaded pocket
O wrap your scarf around my temples
for my face is as cold as a well!

Seafront

Here like the maze of our bewilderment
the thorn-crowned wire spreads high along the shore,
and flowers with rust, and tears our common sun;
and where no paths of love may reach the sea
the shut sands wait deserted for the drowned.

On other islands similarly barbed
mankind lies self-imprisoned in his fear,
and watches through the black sights of a gun
the winging flocks of migratory birds
who cannot speak of freedom, yet are free.

Asleep we are Divided

Asleep we are divided
by worlds our slumbers fashion,
the green stars in my eyes
are the craters of the moon,
and your thick tresses twisting
blue weeds from sweat and darkness
are all the deep primeval seas
I have no power to join.

At last my shuttered eyelids
explode with flint and crystals,
cries from your dreaming tongue
make the walls of sleep fall down,
and in a mineral landscape
I see your body blazing
strange as the world's beginning
and as foreign to my own.

But, as my floating senses
calm down the airs around you
and from these scattered visions
your virtues recollect,
then like a flock of starlings
migrating to their branches
the minutes dress you with your name
and me with leaves of love again.

Poem in the Country

Heron, do not hang over the village
with your wide wings,
do not remind us the sun can be shuttered
with a cross.

The caterpillar leaves the leaf
like a broken house,
and the lake explodes silently
with a barrage of lilies.

The blowing thistle fills the air
with a pattern of warning,
and the mole throws up the dark ground
like a grave.

I take my love to the woods
but she hides her eyes,
I take her among the quarries
but she trembles.

She walks the ruined field
of the distant city,
and weeping searches every stone
for a child's pressed flower.

The Three Winds

The hard blue winds of March
shake the young sheep
and flake the long stone walls;
now from the gusty grass
comes the horned music of rams,
and plovers fall out of the sky
filling their wings with snow.

Tired of this northern tune
the winds turn soft
blowing white butterflies
out of the dog-rose hedges,
and schoolroom songs are full
of boys' green cuckoos
piping the summer round

Till August sends at last
its brick-red breath
over the baking wheat and blistered poppy,
brushing with feathered hands
the skies of brass,
with dreams of river moss
my thirst's delirium.

Equinox

Now tilts the sun his monument,
now sags his raw unwritten stone
deep in October's diamond clay.

And oozy sloes like flies are hung
malignant on the shrivelled stem,
too late to ripen, or to grow.

Now is the time the wasp forsakes
the rose born like a weakly child
of earth-bed's pallor, death-bed's flush.

Time when the gourd upon the ground
cracks open kernel or decay
indifferent to man or worm.

Time of no violence, when at last
the shocked eye clears the battlefield
and burns down black the roots of grass.

And finds the prize of all its pain,
bedded in smoke, on leaves of blood—
love's charcoal cross, unlost, unwon.

Song in the Morning

There are hooked thorns
in the couch of ease
and nails in the floor
of the gentlest chamber.

In your eyes I see
your dead fathers
and your provinces of charm
full of nightingales
or the peonies of my anger.

In your eyes I see
scaffolds of love arising
and the most remote heaven
as familiar as bread.

But even you
mistress of blushing walls
mistress of scarves and painted skins
of oiled walking and intricate obedience,

Cannot seal this tomb
we fashion with our mouths
nor tell which hour vermilion
will prove the first unfaithful.

End of a Season

Out through the numbered doorway of the years,
defiled, and steeped in oils of death,
he sees the lovely season pass
leaving a haunted valley in his bed.

He took with lust the pollen from her lips,
consumed in sleep her fatal grace,
while cries and histories of blood
burned through the cities in the sun.

Across her skies spread out for love
he saw black slaughter shoot its tongue,
he saw the mourners stop their eyes
and crouch among her noisy flowers.

Now staring on the rock of snow
with leaves like prizes in his hand,
he hears the devils chattering in the ice
and cannot wish to see another spring.

Parting

They nourish me who mourn,
they salute me whose hands are starving,
we massacre our eyes with rocks
world has no more to show us.

But why should I lament
and raise lean herds of sorrow
to beat against her
their forsaken tongues?

She has built a tower with my hair
and buried my feet in a well,
shown me her blazing heart
and her star cold heaven.

What though the daylight howls for her
why should I lament?

I see a multitude of deaths
wherein our bones shall creep together
smiling in sheets of similar darkness
joined with a dusty lily evermore.

Poem of Spring and War

In the swift ball of a bird,
in the sepulchre of her mouth
peace lies interred within the tongue's live sheet.

Her eyes unfold the trees
and separate the wind,
but I am blind to her tambourines of spring.

Blind to explosions of blood,
deaf to the shots that pass
through legs of grass from batteries of rain.

The young brain of the year
is wrapped within a skin
of alternating fear and desperate embraces,

But the races of the earth
are solitary as islands,
their rivers of hands and lips drawn back from
     the sea.

Love, you are free to hide
in the thighs of the crooked slain,
under lids of pain, or breasts of memorial brass.

Or free to pass your strength
from a bullet's sudden grip
to hold the length of a scream within your sight.

But night is no longer a girl,
and spring is only a bed
for the icy dead, and the fury of the living.

Interval

All day the purple battle of love
as scented mouths position
soft fields of contesting langour
or jealous peaks of suspicion.

All day the trumpeting of fingers,
the endless march of desire
across the continent of an eyelid
or the desert of a hair.

How long we roam these territories
trailing our twin successes,
till the bending sun collapses
and I escape your kisses.

Then I drink the night like a coconut
and earth regains its shape;
at last the eunuch's neutral dream
and the beardless touch of sleep.

Deliverance

Through naked sticks, his winter bones,
   The dead wind blew the snow,
Man was the scaffold of disaster,
   The trembling net of woe.

His starving veins were frozen strings,
   They rigged his skeleton,
The hailstones cracked his tattered skins
   But could not drive him on.

His howling eyeballs could not know,
   Searching the dreadful night,
Which gleam was star, or scimitar,
   Or which the beacon light.

He thought: 'I am the cage of pain,
   A trap for every sorrow,
Yet one day, as I comb this storm,
   Shall I not catch the swallow?'

The black wind drops, at last the sun
   With green dust beats the air,
His hands and skull with blossoms fill,
   His crown sprouts grassy hair.

His sick veins now do spring alive,
   Leaves run along each bone,
And in his hollow eyes the birds
   Sing out for him alone.

Trimmed like a lamp and warm with love
  He shouts his noisy blood,
No sound recalls that age of grief,
  No memory doubts this Good.

Village of Winter Carols

Village of winter carols
and gawdy spinning tops,
of green-handed walnuts
and games in the moon.

You were adventure's web,
the flag of fear I flew
riding black stallions
through the rocky streets.

You were the first faint map
of the mysterious sun,
chart of my island flesh
and the mushroom-tasting kiss.

But no longer do I join
your children's sharp banditti,
nor seek the glamour of
your ravished apples.

Your hillocks build no more
their whales and pyramids,
nor howl across the night
their springing wolves.

For crouching in my brain
the crafty thigh of love
twists your old landscape
with a new device.

And every field has grown
a strange and flowering pit
where I must try the blind
and final trick of youth.

Diversion

Again, it seems, the wind turns soft about us
and from the lobbing sun's oblique grenade
a shaft of scent or splintered light thrown up
assails the iron sleep our senses wear,
until compassion like an old wound wakes us
and dazed we stand among the diving birds.

Within this piteous, bursting air of March,
war's like a boulder on the primrose shoot,
while every finger, harnessed to a gun,
fumbles for love, and every trigger-touch
curling for death, still trembles to enclose
the human rose the target of its wish.

Yet this we fear, it knows no line or bastion,
no bluff of armoured cage or sunken cave;
crouched in the earth, impaled upon the sky,
made blind or deaf by anger's mutilation
O still we hear it plotting in our hearts
to break their walls at last with love or reason.

But comes the battled night our conscience dies,
the voice of war returns to blast our dream:
'Ignore the waxing crocus, crack the oak,
march through the choking meadows stiff with blood
and catch the Foe upon a naked thorn;
your ears are traitors listening to the spring,
your pity is a hostage bound and dumb.'

Milkmaid

The girl's far treble, muted to the heat,
calls like a fainting bird across the fields
to where her flock lies panting for her voice,
their black horns buried deep in marigolds.

They climbed awake, like drowsy butterflies,
and press their red flanks through the tall branched grass,
and as they go their wandering tongues embrace
the vacant summer mirrored in their eyes.

Led to the limestone shadows of a barn
they snuff their past embalmèd in the hay,
while her cool hand, cupped to the udder's fount,
distils the brimming harvest of their day.

Look what a cloudy cream the earth gives out,
fat juice of buttercups and meadow-rye;
the girl dreams milk within her body's field
and hears, far off, her muted children cry.

Guest of Honour

I do not think I shall ever again
behold the sun so mighty
so golden his loins of light,
I shall never again feel as I do now
his flame-haired pulse pounding the writhing air
as if the world would break
or bleed,
or bear all man's desire.

Nor shall I ever again be so aware
of the green world's womb
pierced to infinity as now I see it,
where all its life spilled out upon my lap
pulls me with plaintive claws,
while bitter soils come close against my mouth
to feed the single summer that is mine.

For this ripe chance is cast against my promise;
the landscape's instant smile,
lighting my chosen eye no past could blind,
now shows beneath its bloom a deadlier prize,
a field of wounds shocking my expectation
where men grown drunk with burning cups of pain
feast on the poisons they must offer me.

So life is won – but not its celebration;
there'll be no games of love,
triumphs of sweat, or towers built to the moon,
all this I must accept.
But keep me, God, from any trivial rage,
let me exploit time's brute coincidence
to know a generation by its loss.
But let me not revile it for my loss.

No, I shall never again, alas,
behold the sun so mighty
striding the ruined or the ready world,
yet I take heed;
for to his loins of still enduring light
shall mount that luckier child of peace, who must
the eager but eccentric future try,
whose course my gift, but not my curse, can sway.

Guadalquivir

Here on this desert plain
the fields are dust,
strangled by wind,
burnt by the quicklime sun.

But where the river's tongue
scoops out its channel deep
across the iron land
trees grow, and leaves
of splendid green
force back the baking air.

Fish and small birds
do strike with diamond mouths
the windows of the water,
while memories of song
and flowers flow
along the slender cables
of the mud.

So to the wires of love
do my limbs leap,
so does your finger draw
across my arid breast
torrents of melting snow
on threads of seed.

The Wild Trees

O the wild trees of my home,
forests of blue dividing the pink moon,
the iron blue of those ancient branches
with their berries of vermilion stars.

In that place of steep meadows
the stacked sheaves are roasting,
and the sun-torn tulips
are tinders of scented ashes.

But here I have lost
the dialect of your hills,
my tongue has gone blind
far from their limestone roots.

Through trunks of black elder
runs a fox like a lantern,
and the hot grasses sing
with the slumber of larks.

But here there are thickets
of many different gestures,
torn branches of brick and steel
frozen against the sky.

O the wild trees of home
with their sounding dresses,
locks powdered with butterflies
and cheeks of blue moss.

I want to see you rise
from my brain's dry river,
I want your lips of wet roses
laid over my eyes.

O fountains of earth and rock,
gardens perfumed with cucumber,
home of secret valleys
where the wild trees grow.

Let me return at last
to your fertile wilderness,
to sleep with the coiled fernleaves
in your heart's live stone.

The Multitudinous Lamp

Sunlight breaks it does not bleed
it knows the close laugh of the leaves
it fits the pigeon's every feather
it is the skin on every hand

it is the tongue that sucks the shore
the muscle in the water's sleeve
the forest of a maiden's hair
the dance that twists the empty street

it flays the shout within my mouth
it grins across my sacred grief
it leads me on a frightened string
and spits obscenely on my grave

it is the flower pinned to the wind
the convict screaming in his cell
blood hills, the bitterness of dawn,
the thousand journeys from thy bed.

River

The morning is white
with the hot frost of elder,
blizzards of scent
blind the shuddering walls.

The red flames of lizards
wriggle out of the ditches
to suck the black tar
from the smoking road.

There is thirst on my tongue
like the powder of fungus,
my throat is a sandstorm
of thistle and moth.

O where is the river
and where are the willows,
your kisses of hazel
to sweeten my mouth?

You are that stream
where the glass fish dazzle
the flash of their scales
on the star-blue stones.

The heart of cool amber
in baking granite,
the motionless lily
in pools of clay.

Dewdrop of honey,
moisture of bloom,
in the sweating rose
and the branded poppy.

O bring me your river,
your moss-green bridges,
the bank of your breasts
with their hill-cold springs;

The voice of the moorhen
diving under your eyelids
and your ankles like swans
in a nest of reeds. . . .

The Long War

Less passionate the long war throws
its burning thorn about all men,
caught in one grief, we share one wound,
and cry one dialect of pain.

We have forgot who fired the house,
whose easy mischief spilt first blood,
under one raging roof we lie
the fault no longer understood.

But as our twisted arms embrace
the desert where our cities stood,
death's family likeness in each face
must show, at last, our brotherhood.